W9-AEY-801

DISCARD

Markham Public Library
Milliken Mills Branch
7600 Kennedy Road, Unit 1
Markham, ON L3R 9R5

People of Importance

ALBERT EINSTEIN: Great Scientist

Anne Marie Sullivan   Giuliano Ferri

Mason Crest

If the Theory of Relativity is correct, the Germans will say I'm a German, and the French will say I'm a citizen of the world. However, if my theories are wrong, the French will say I'm a German, and the Germans will say I'm a Jew.

—Albert Einstein

During his life, Albert Einstein was a citizen of three different countries: Germany, Switzerland and the United States of America. He made this comment during World War II, when he was trying to find a safe place to live. Although he was born in Germany, he later moved to Switzerland and became a Swiss citizen. He was also Jewish. He felt threatened by the Nazis and decided to move to America during the war. By that time, he was already one of the most famous scientists in the world. He was invited everywhere to work and lecture. Einstein truly was a citizen of the world.

Some of the most brilliant minds in the history of mankind got off to a slow start. Abraham Lincoln, Sir Isaac Newton—certainly no one would have singled them out as budding geniuses early on. In fact, people thought they were slow to learn when they were children. Albert Einstein was this kind of child.

He was born in Germany in 1879. His father, along with his uncle, owned a small electronics factory there. Albert was odd looking as a child. His head was very large for his body. At five years old, he only spoke a few words. He liked to be alone and showed little interest in the games and toys most children loved. His mother started to worry that there might be something wrong with him.

No one could see what was going on inside Albert's head. His lips were silent, but his curious eyes noticed everything. He didn't seem interested in doing anything, but his mind never stopped moving. There is no way to find out what he was thinking about back then. But maybe he seemed so slow because his thoughts were so deep.

Although he did eventually learn to talk, Albert remained quiet. He rarely ran and played with other children. Instead, he loved to build big castles with blocks or make tall, fragile towers of cards.

He doesn't seem like other children.

Nonsense! He'll be fine.

One day when he was five, Albert was sick and had to stay in bed. To pass the time, he played with a compass his father brought to amuse him. Albert was delighted. He turned the compass around and around, staring fascinated at the red needle that always pointed in the same direction, no matter what he tried. "Why is this?" he asked himself. "Is there some powerful, invisible force pushing this needle?"

As he thought, it came to Albert that everyday things were hiding many secrets. There were so many things that people didn't know. He longed to uncover these secrets. This small compass needle guided Albert towards a lifetime of questioning. Albert's questioning pointed all people towards a new understanding of the universe.

Why does the needle always point the same way?

Because the earth has a magnetic power that pulls the needle north.

When Albert was little, many boys dreamed of becoming soldiers. They worshiped these tall, strong men in their smart uniforms. Not Albert. Everything about the army frightened him.

The soldiers used to parade along the city streets, with music playing and weapons glinting at their sides. Excited by this grand spectacle, children would follow the parade clapping and cheering.

But the soldiers marching in perfect step and the sight of their cold, sharp weapons terrified Albert. School was too much like the army.

When Albert started school, he found that the most important thing was to follow orders well. The school decided what to teach and made sure every student was taught the same thing and took the same tests. Doing well in school meant putting the right answers in the right boxes. It didn't matter whether the students really enjoyed what they were learning or understood what they were taught.

Albert hated this system. He thought the school treated its students like farm animals: if fed the same amount of food, they should all grow to the same size. When he talked about his schooling, Albert said, "Even a healthy beast with a healthy appetite will lose its taste for food, no matter how good it is, if it is forced to eat when it is not hungry."

School is a place for learning.

It feels more like an army camp.

This kind of education stifled the imagination. Albert once said, "Imagination is more important than knowledge." He was very unhappy and grew even quieter in school. He refused to repeat things he did not believe, so he chose not to speak. His classmates and teachers decided he must be stupid and thought him timid and strange.

His mother loved music. When Albert was six, she hired a violin teacher for him. At first, he didn't like the discipline of learning music. He had to practise the same things over and over again. There was no other way to become skillful with the fingering and the bow, but he felt like a machine.

One day he heard someone else playing *A Little Night Music* by Mozart. He thought it sounded so beautiful and realised that music was a way to express what was inside him. From that day on, he practised much harder. He loved his violin and took it everywhere.

Albert's Uncle Jacob introduced him to another of his loves, mathematics. Uncle Jacob found ways to make algebra interesting and exciting. He turned it into a game, telling Albert to imagine that he was hunting in the woods, searching for the right answers. Albert loved math when it was presented to him like this. "Interest is the best teacher," he later said. Soon he found he loved nothing better than hunting down the right answers.

Every Thursday, Albert's family invited Max Talmud, a poor student at at Munich University, to dinner. Max always brought Albert books on nature, astronomy, math and other interesting subjects. In these books, Albert found answers to many of his questions. He learned why the compass needle always points north, where rainbows come from and much more.

Knowing things surprised and delighted Albert. Knowledge made him feel like a bird. He could soar high above the world, seeing and understanding everything below.

Albert's family moved to Italy when he was 15 because his father's business failed. They left Albert in Germany to finish his schooling. He was so unhappy that he convinced his doctor to write a note saying he should go home for the sake of his health. Before he had a chance to turn in his doctor's note, the school asked him to leave.

In Italy Albert's family let him read and explore whatever he pleased. His parents were surprised to discover that their quiet boy wouldn't stop talking about the things that interested him.

Albert loved to walk in the hills near a lake with his sister. As he gazed down on the reflections in the lake, he began wondering about light. It was a fascinating mystery. How did it move—in waves like water, or in particles like dust? How fast did it travel? What would happen if people could move at the speed of light? Could they chase light? If so, what would happen? The questions this young boy was asking would one day change the world.

My ideas about light were more powerful than anything I learned in school.

When he was 16, Albert went to a university in Switzerland. After he graduated, it took Albert more than a year to find a job. It was a cold, hungry year for him. Finally, the Swiss Patent Office hired him as a patent examiner, testing other people's new inventions. Now that he was earning a salary, he decided he could get married. He married Milena Marie in 1903.

When he wasn't working at the patent office, Albert continued his research. He still wanted to know what would happen if you chased light at the speed of light. The University of Zurich awarded him a doctorate degree, the highest degree anyone can earn, in 1905. He published three papers that same year. In them, he introduced his new ideas to the world, including his special theory of relativity. Einstein's theory of relativity has become one of the most famous scientific ideas of all time. By publishing these papers, a Swiss patent examiner changed scientists' ideas about time and space forever.

One of the most important figures in the history of science is Sir Isaac Newton. The entire body of knowledge called physics was based on his ideas. He imagined the universe as a perfectly balanced clock.

And why not? After so many successes had been built on Newton's ideas, arguing with him would be tough. But Albert realised he would have to disagree with Isaac Newton, who had been dead for 200 years. "Nature is a heartless, unsympathetic judge," Albert once said. "It never says a theory is correct." Newton's laws could explain most things. But scientists in the 1800s were uncovering events in nature that slipped through cracks in Newton's clockwork universe.

For Newton, time and space were two different things. They acted separately, and one didn't affect the other. He also thought time and space never changed. Albert wasn't so sure. He thought they might change depending on who was looking at them.

For example, suppose one person sees two things happening at the exact same time. Another person, standing in a different place but looking at these same two events, might see them happen at two different times.

The universe looks different from different points of view.

The universe is like a clock.

Imagine a moving train with a lamp in the middle of the car. This lamp can send light in two opposite directions at the same time. The train has special doors that open when the light hits them. When the lamp is turned on, the light shines on both the front and back doors of the train car and opens them.

To a man sitting on the train under the lamp, the doors seem to open at the same time. But to another person standing outside the train, the back door appears to open before the front door. Why is this?

The train is moving forward. Although everything inside the train is moving along with it, to the man inside, everything feels like it's standing still. Because he moves at the same speed as the train, he feels like he is sitting still and only the train is moving. The doors, which appear to be staying in one place, seem to open at the same time.

To someone outside the train, everything in the train looks like it is moving forward, including both doors. The light travels at the same speed towards both doors. But the back door is moving towards the light, while the front door is moving away from it. So the light hits the back door first. From outside the train, the back door opens first. Time changes, depending on where you are and how fast you are travelling.

Some people began wondering what Albert's ideas might mean in real life. They imagined a set of twins. One twin remains here on earth, while the other travels into space on a rocket that moves at the speed of light. What would happen if this twin returned to earth 40 years later? He had been travelling at the speed of light all that time. For him, time had slowed down. The twin who remained on earth would be 40 years older. But what of the twin who had been moving all that time? Would he still be a young man? Since people cannot travel at the speed of light, there is no way to test this idea. But it is fun to ask the question.

Hi, Dad,
I'm home!

I'm not Dad! i'm
your brother!

Albert also believed that the sun's gravity pulls the light from stars, so it does not travel in a straight line. His ideas about gravity seemed impossible to prove. But in 1919, British scientists watched a total eclipse of the sun from two different places on the earth, Africa and Brazil. From what they observed, they could tell that light was curved as it passed by the sun. So there was the proof! These results caused a sensation, and Albert became a hero among scientists.

In 1921, Albert received the Nobel Prize for Physics, one of the greatest honours in the world for a scientist. But the award was not given for his discovery of relativity. Instead, it was given for another idea in one of his papers from 1905. In this paper, he described something called the photoelectric effect: when light hits some kinds of metal, electricity is given off. Albert proposed that light is made of particles called photons, a completely new idea. Albert's ideas in this paper laid the groundwork for a new kind of physics and led to the discovery of nuclear energy.

Albert's wife took their children to live in Switzerland while he stayed behind in Germany. After five years, they were divorced. Eventually, Albert would marry his cousin, Elsa.

I love science best of all.

I'm leaving.

A long time ago, people in some places imagined the world riding on the back of a giant turtle.

About 100 years before Isaac Newton was born, the scientists Copernicus and Galileo realised that the earth travels around the sun. Many people were very angry with them for arguing that the earth is not the centre of the universe. Copernicus and Galileo believed that the universe is centred around the sun.

The ancient Greek scientist Aristotle was the first to believe that the earth is a sphere. He thought that the earth was the centre of the universe.

Isaac Newton said the universe has no centre. It goes on forever. The planets travel in the same circles forever because they are held to the stars by gravity.

Albert Einstein said the universe might not go on forever. It may be a closed space. But it can be travelled forever without ever reaching an edge because space and time are curved by gravity. A circle has no beginning and no end, so it can be travelled without end.

Which is right?

Gravity is a force.

Gravity is a bending of space and time.

During World War II, scientists used Einstein's theory to build the atomic bomb. At the end of World War II, America dropped the bomb on two Japanese cities, killing thousands of people.

Albert was overcome with grief. Even though he didn't invent or decide to use the bomb, he felt that the death and destruction in Japan were partly his fault. He spent the rest of his life speaking out against the bomb and working for world peace.

Albert spoke up for what he believed, but he never wanted to take part in politics. He was asked to become the leader of Israel, the new Jewish country formed after World War II, but he said no. He preferred to stick with what he loved: science. He moved to America, and until he died in 1955, Albert remained at Princeton University doing his research.

People remember Albert as a wise, caring man who was full of humour. It is hard to believe he was once mistaken for a slow, strange child. Albert could tell that the universe was more than it seemed to be. He taught us to look harder and deeper.

His life can teach us a lesson about people as well. When they seem strange, maybe they are just refusing to be ordinary. When they seem too quiet, maybe they are just thinking very hard. Sometimes we have to look harder and deeper, like Albert did.

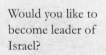

Would you like to become leader of Israel?

No, thank you. Politics change, but science lasts forever.

BIOGRAPHY

Author Anne Marie Sullivan received her Bachelor of Arts in English from Temple University. She has worked in the publishing field as a writer and editor. She lives with her husband and three children in the Philadelphia suburbs.

Mason Crest
450 Parkway Drive, Suite D
Broomall, PA 19008
www.masoncrest.com

Copyright © 2014 by Mason Crest, an imprint of National Highlights, Inc. All rights reserved. No part of this publication may be reproduced or transmitted in any form or by any means, electronic or mechanical, including photocopying, recording, taping or any information storage and retrieval system, without permission from the publisher.

Printed and bound in the United States of America.

First printing
9 8 7 6 5 4 3 2 1

Series ISBN: 978-1-4222-2839-5
ISBN: 978-1-4222-2840-1
ebook ISBN: 978-1-4222-8960-0

The Library of Congress has cataloged the
        hardcopy format(s) as follows:

            Library of Congress Cataloging-in-Publication Data

Sullivan, Anne Marie.
  Albert Einstein : great scientist / Anne Marie Sullivan.
      p. cm. — (People of importance)
  Audience: 009.
  Audience: Grades 4 to 6.
  ISBN 978-1-4222-2840-1 (hardcover) — ISBN 978-1-4222-2839-5 (series) — ISBN 978-1-4222-8960-0 (ebook)
  1. Einstein, Albert, 1879-1955—Juvenile literature. 2. Physicists—Biography—Juvenile literature. I. Title.
  QC16.E5S85 2014
  530.092—dc23
                              2013005808

Produced by Vestal Creative Services.
www.vestalcreative.com
Illustrations copyright © 1998 Giuliano Ferri.